VICTORY PARADE
The Lisbon Lions are given a hero's welcome as they tour Celtic Park with the European Cup

CEL

EUROPEAN ADVENTURES

FROM Lisbon to Barcelona, Celtic's legend has been built on a foundation of famous wins on foreign shores and this is the ultimate celebration of the Bhoys in Europe.

Take a stroll down memory lane as we relive the greatest nights in Celtic's sensational history - all captured through the lens of history.

This is a picture story of the club's greatest triumphs in the European arena. From the early days and the first steps into the continental battleground to the domination of the 60s and 70s under Jock Stein and the glory of that famous May night in the Estadio Nacional in 1967.

After Lisbon, we scale the heights again only to falter at the final hurdle in Milan against Feyenoord but the dream lives on through the 70s.

From there, follow the fortunes through the 80s and 90s to the Champions League nights of the early naughties and the rebirth of Celtic as a modern force.

The story of Seville and the amazing run to the 2003 UEFA Cup final is told in detail and then we come full circle to the famous night in November 2012 when Lionel Messi and the best club side in the world were downed in delirious Paradise.

Celtic. More than just a club. And this is more than just a picture book.

Editor: Austin Barrett

Picture Research:
Brian Gallagher and Julie Bryceland

Cover Design:
Bill Sullivan

Design & Production:
Ryan McGraw, Bill Sullivan, Graeme Thomson, Kevin McAllion, Fraser Glen, Paul Watson

Marketing & Circulation:
Tom Heffernan and Margaret Hoisington

IN THE BEGINNING –
THE SWINGING SIXTIES

SKIPPING TO GLORY Celtic players lap the track in preparation for their European Cup Winners' Cup campaign in 1963

EVERY story has a beginning, every journey has a first step. And for Celtic's European adventure, that was a flight to Spain in September 1962 for a Fairs Cup tie against Valencia.

Five years later, the club would scale a summit of Everest proportions 550 miles across the Portuguese border but Valencia would prove to be their base camp for that climb to Europe's peak.

Jimmy McGrory's men were beaten 4-2, with Bobby Carroll notching a double, and Valencia completed a 6-4 aggregate win back in Glasgow on their way to retaining the trophy.

The following season Celtic reached the Cup Winners' Cup semi-finals, with John Hughes becoming the first Hoops player to score a hat-trick in Europe wi a treble against Basel.

But they learned a hard lesson in the last four when, after a glorious 3-0 win

THE CLASS OF '62 The Parkhead pioneers who took the club's first step into Europe

LAPPING IT UP
Billy McNeill and keeper Frank Haffey return to pitch after the challenge game against Real as the fans demand a lap of honour from their side, even in defeat. After the match the great Ferenc Puskas sang the praises of McNeill and Paddy Crerard

first leg over MTK Budapest, they ...ped 4-0 in Hungary.
...1966, a certain Jock Stein had found ...ay into the dugout and the club lost ... more in the Cup Winners' Cup semis. ...th Liverpool leading 2-0 at Anfield ...2-1 on aggregate, Bobby Lennox had a ...wrongly ruled out for offside. ...obbed Celtic off a final at home in ...gow but they were to take their ...nge on a loftier stage a year later...

SET UP FOR A FALL
Billy McNeill exchanges pennants before the first leg of the Cup Winners' Cup semi with MTK Budapest in 1964, a match the Hoops go on to win 3-0. But their hopes of reaching a first final are dashed in the return as the Hungarians romp to a 4-0 win

PEST FOOT FORWARD
Stevie Chalmers collides with MTK keeper Ferenc Kovalik during the first leg in Glasgow

BAD OMEN
McNeill and John Hughes choose a book called Murder Revisited for the flight to Budapest

CELTIC v. REAL MADRID
CHALLENGE MATCH
BLUE AND WHITE TROPHY
2/6
CELTIC PARK
MONDAY, 10th SEPT., 1962
Kick-off 7 p.m.

YOUR "WIN-A-CAR" NUMBER IS
See Page 7

A REAL EDUCATION
Francisco Gento seals a 3-1 win for European champions Real Madrid in a fund-raising challenge match at Parkhead in September 1962

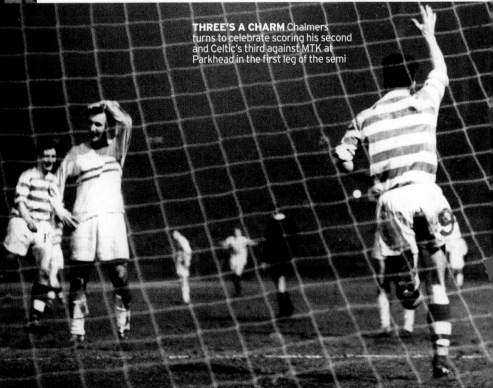

THREE'S A CHARM Chalmers turns to celebrate scoring his second and Celtic's third against MTK at Parkhead in the first leg of the semi

08 CELTIC
EUROPEAN ADVENTURES

THE SWINGING SIXTIES

KEEP THEM SHOUT LAD Keeper John Fallon barks orders to a defence that includes future Lisbon Lions McNeill, John Clark and Tom Gemmell as Celtic win 1-0 Bratislava to complete a 2- aggregate success over Slovan in the 1964 Cup Winners' Cup

POP UP Skipper McNeill shakes hands with Slovan's Jan Popluhar in the win at Parkhead

CHALM DOWN
Steve Chalmers is fouled by Slovan keeper Viliam Schrojf and defender Jozef Filo, giving Bobby Murdoch the chance to seal a 1-0 first-leg win from the spot

BRATS MINE Ian Young cleares the danger for Celtic in Bratislava as McNeill and Clark look on. John Hughes then seals the 2-0 aggregate triumph in style by running half the field before scoring a sensational solo goal

NO PAIN NO GAIN Murdoch fights off concussion to help seal a 3-0 win over Dinamo Zagreb in 1963, dashing the pre-match optimism of Zlatko Markovic, Zdenko Kobescak, Slaven Zambata and Rudolf Belin

NO RAINING ON THE PARADE Only 8,000 fans turn out at Parkhead to see the Hoops take on Basel in 1963 due to heavy rain but they miss a barrage of goals as a 5-0 win seals a 10-1 aggregate triumph

BHOYS ARE DINAMITE Goal hero Chalmers takes the acclaim as his double helps seal victory over Zagreb at Parkhead, paving the way for a 4-2 aggregate win in the Cup Winners' Cup second round

BUSMAN'S HOLIDAY Charlie Gallacher Willie O'Neill and Murdoch do their homework on Portugal ahead of a 1964 Fairs Cup tie with Leixoes, with Celtic drawing 1-1 after having Ian Young and Chalmers sent off

SORE LOSERS English ref Ernie Crawford struggles to control the ill-disciplined Leixoes players in a towsy second leg that the Hoops win 3-0 with 10 men after Charlie Gallacher has to limp off following a bad tackle in the days when there were no subs. The Portuguese players then walk off to boos from the crowd, above, after giving the Celtic fans a glimpse of European football's darker side

NOU RIVALS
Billy McNeill welcomes Nou Camp skipper Ferran Olivella to Parkhead before the second leg of the 1964 Fairs Cup clash

Bienvenido a Glasgow el C. de F. Barcelona

C.F.B.

FAIRS CITIES CUP
SECOND ROUND—SECOND LEG

OFFICIAL
Illustrated Souvenir Programme
PRICE - - 1/-

CELTIC
v.
BARCELONA

at
CELTIC PARK, WEDNESDAY, DECEMBER 2, 1964
KICK-OFF 7.30 p.m.

TEARS FOR SOUVENIRS
Jimmy Johnstone and fan Jon Coll, below, arriv back with gifts after losing 3-1 to Barcelona in t first leg of the 1964 Fairs Cup tie but the Hoops left empty handed at home as they can only dra 0-0 in the return. They aren't helped when Stev Chalmers limps off, left, leaving them with 10 m and John Hughes angers Barca, above, after gi keeper Salvador Sadurni a shoulder charge

JOKE BOYS, WE'LL RULE EUROPE SOON Celtic boss Jock Stein enjoys a laugh with his squad as they prepare for his first match in charge in March 1965

BRINGING HOME THE DANISH BACON Aarhus keeper Bent Martin punches clear from Joe McBride in 1965, above, while Ronnie Simpson gathers at the other end as Celtic beat the Danes 2-0 at Parkhead to win 3-0 on aggregate in the Cup Winners' Cup

CELTIC
V
LIVERPOOL
14TH APRIL
1966

FLY BHOYS The Hoops head out to face Dinamo Kiev in 1966 after Murdoch seals a 3-0 win at home, below, and McNeill jokes with fan before 1-1 draw in return leg

FIRST BATTLE OF BRITAIN McNeill and Ron Yeats shake hands ahead of the Cup Winners' Cup semi-final with Liverpool, far left, and Celts celebrate a 1-0 home win thanks to Chalmers, below left. But it all goes wrong in the return as Tommy Gemmell picks up the ball after Tommy Smith's opener, below, and fans throw bottles, left, as the Hoops lose 2-0

CHAPTER 2 –
THE ROAD TO LISBON

DUKLA DUMPED Celtic players and backroom staff celebrate after a 0-0 draw in Prague puts them in the 1967 European Cup final

CELTIC
EUROPEAN ADVENTURES

THE ROAD TO LISBON

FRENCH BLISS McNeill welcomes Nantes skipper Robert Budzynski to Parkhead before Chalmers nets Celtic's second, top, as they seal a 6-1 aggregate win on the night 'Flying Flea' Johnstone, above, was grounded

ZURICH, Nantes, Novi Sad, Prague. It's not the standard route from Glasgow to Lisbon but, then again, Celtic's 1967 European campaign was far from standard.

And when you're conquering a continent, it's always best to take the scenic route.

First up were Swiss champions Zurich and Celtic won 2-0 in Glasgow thanks to Tommy Gemmell and Joe McBride before sending shockwaves across Europe by winning 3-0 in the return, with Gemmell netting either side of a Stevie Chalmers goal. A trip to France looked fraught with danger in round two but Stein's men came from a goal behind to win 3-1 thanks to goals from McBride, Chalmers and Bobby Lennox.

The French press tagged Jimmy Johnstone 'The Flying Flea' and the winger netted in the return, with further goals from Chalmers and Lennox sealing another 3-1 win.

The Bhoys walked on, with hope in their hearts, to a meeting with Vojvodina of Yugoslavia. They turned in a fine defensive display in the first leg in Novi Sad but lost 1-0. The second leg was the stuff of legend as Chalmers drew them level and with a play-off beckoning in neutral Rotterdam, Billy McNeill rose in injury-time to bury a header.

Dukla Prague were all that stood in the way of Celtic and the final now.

An early Johnstone goal put Stein's side ahead at Parkhead only for Dukla to level but Willie Wallace struck twice to cap a 3-1 first-leg success.

An ultra defensive display then sealed a 0-0 draw in the return but the end justified the means. Lisbon and a date with destiny beckoned.

CESAR CONQUERS McNeill threatens Vojvodina in the quarter-final, below, before celebrating his winner, left, to leave the Hoops jubilant after 2-1 aggregate success, below left, as Chalmers swaps jerseys with a gutted opponent

ALMOST THERE Jimmy Johnstone, left, takes the fight to Dukla in the first leg and Stevie Chalmers comes close with a header, below, as the Hoops win 3-1 before skipper Billy McNeill fears for a fallen comrade in Prague, above

CELTIC'S BRAVEHEART
Stanislav Strunc silences Parkhead with the leveller, above, but Celts win thanks to two goals from Willie Wallace, who battles Ladislav Novak, left, and keeper Ivo Viktor, top

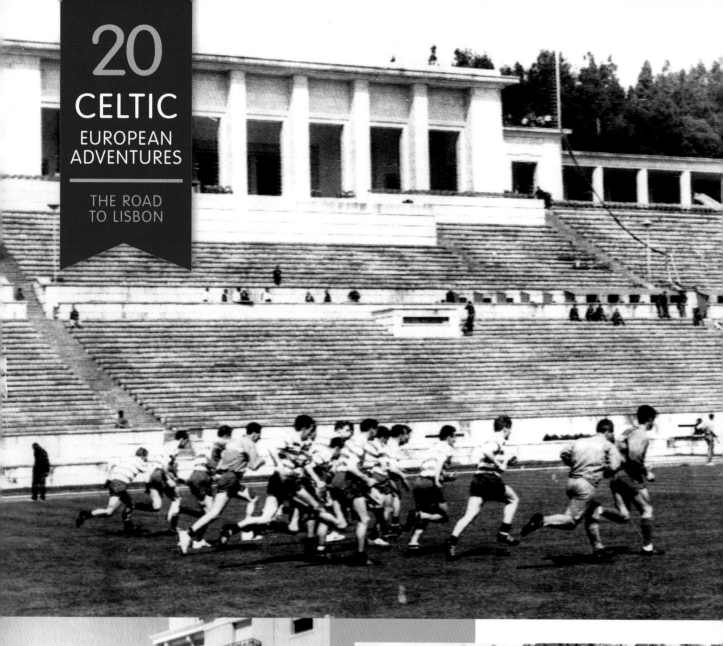

READY FOR OUR DAY IN THE SUN Manager Jock Stein puts his stars through their paces at the Estadio Nacional, above and top, before John Clark, Billy McNeill, Berti Auld, Willie Wallace and Stevie Chalmers relax at the hotel pool, left

ROADS LEAD TO LISBON Hoops fans descend on the Portuguese capital in their droves for the biggest game in the club's history and quickly make nselves feel right at home upon arrival, settling down at roadside bars and cafes for a few beers, above left, as they soak up the sun and atmosphere

CHAPTER 3 -
LISBON: DAY OF GLORY

HAIL, HAIL CESAR Victorious skipper Billy McNeill is mobbed by fans at the final whistle in Lisbon as assistant boss Sean Fallon looks on

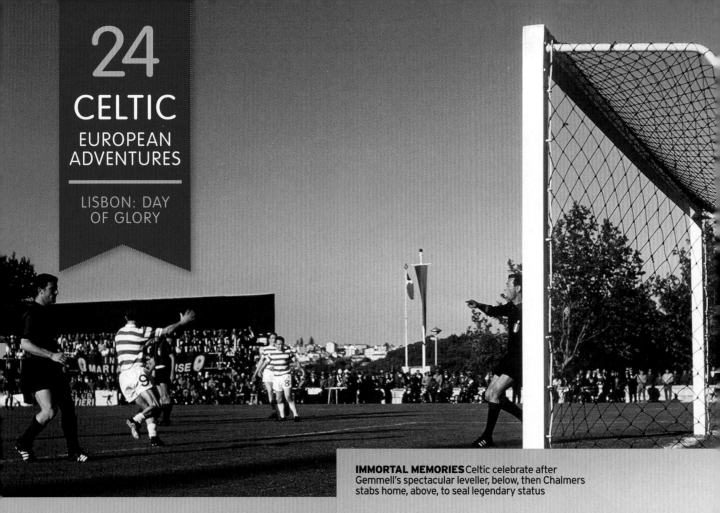

IMMORTAL MEMORIES Celtic celebrate after Gemmell's spectacular leveller, below, then Chalmers stabs home, above, to seal legendary status

THE wee Glaswegian sauntered his way to the customs desk at Glasgow Airport on Friday, May 26, 1967. Just off the flight from Lisbon with a grin as wide as the Clyde, he held a carrier bag which clanked and swayed in the same direction as he did.

"Anything to declare, sir?" the agent behind the counter asked. "Huv ye no heard, big yin?" came the reply. "Celtic 2 Inter Milan 1."

And with that, our man skipped off into the night. He did not walk alone.

In the hours just after Celtic's remarkable triumph, supporters around the world celebrated but even at the height of their revelry, few could have imagined the magnitude of what their team had achieved.

At the first attempt, Celtic had become the first British team to win the European Cup with a team born inside a 30-mile radius of Celtic Park. They also won it in a manner that flew in the face of the ultra-defensive style of play so favoured by the dominant Latin clubs.

Celtic were given little or no chance against the Italians and their wily coach Helenio Herrera.

But if Herrera had heard Stein's pre-match press conference, he may have already known his superstars had no chance. "We are going to attack as we have never attacked before," said Stein. "Cups are not won by individuals. They are won by men in a team, men who put their club before personal prestige. I am lucky – I have the players who do just that for Celtic."

And so it proved. Celtic were so good on the day, they even could afford to give Inter a goal of a start. But Sandro Mazzola's penalty, although it kept Inter in the lead for nearly 70 minutes, proved an irrelevance.

Tommy Gemmell's screamer and a clever Stevie Chalmers finish won the cup in the last 15 minutes, not just for Celtic but for football fans around the globe. Defensive tactics had suffered a fatal blow.

The Lisbon Lions were born. And for Celtic fans, their roars echo through eternity.

UNDER SIEGE
Inter goalie Giuliar Sarti is relieved af a Chalmers effort comes back off his

SILVER SERVICE
Billy McNeill proudly shows off the
European Cup to cap a perfect season for
Celts after a domestic clean sweep

PARTY ON THE PARK
Jubilant Hoops fans race on to the pitch at
full-time to hail their heroes, top, with
skipper McNeill, left, and Willie Wallace,
above, among the first to be mobbed

FIELD OF DREAMS
Within moments of the full-time whistle the pitch at the Estadio Nacional becomes a sea of green and white as Celtic fans savour their finest moment

BASKING IN THE GLORY McNeill and Bobby Murdoch bring out the European Cup back at Celtic Park before Matt Busby presents Jock Stein with the BBC's Team of the Year prize at the Sports Review

LAP DANCING
Stein's heroes take the acclaim of a packed Parkhead as they go on a lap of honour with the European Cup

KEEP ON TRUCKING
The Lisbon Lions just can't keep their hands off the European Cup as they take it for a spin

PRIZE FIGHTERS Stein shows off the trophies won in 1967 while Ronnie Simpson takes a closer look at the European Cup plaque during a meeting with Lord Provost John Johnston, above

CHAPTER 4 – THE SEVENTIES

MADRID MAD MEN Chaos erupts at the end of the brutal first-leg European Cup semi-final between Celtic and Atletico Madrid in 1974. The Spaniards had three players sent off after using disgusting tactics in a 0-0 draw

CELTIC would pick up in the Seventies where they left off in the Sixties, dominating the European scene. But they could never quite scale the heights of 1967 again.

A glance at their European record from September 1963 to April 1974 makes staggering reading. Across three competitions, Celtic played in two finals, six semi-finals and eight quarter-finals.

As the new decade dawned, Jock Stein would go as close as ever to repeating his triumph in Lisbon as Celtic swept to a second European Cup final.

The second-leg triumph over Don Revie's Leeds was the highlight of the decade. Watched by 136,505 people, which remains a record for a UEFA competition, Celtic came from 1-0 down to win 2-1 on the night and seal a 3-1 aggregate triumph thanks to goals from John Hughes and Bobby Murdoch.

Sadly, the joy was short-lived as Feyenoord won the final 2-1 in Milan after extra-time. As Billy McNeill remarked years later: "It was like we climbed the mountain and fell over the hill at the top."

Season 71/72 would see Celtic reach the semis again only for Inter to exact a measure of revenge for 1967 with a penalty shoot-out win in Glasgow.

Perhaps the most disappointing episode of the Seventies came in April 1974 when Celtic took on Atletico Madrid in another semi-final.

Atletico had three men sent off and seven booked in a farcical first leg which saw Jimmy Johnstone assaulted from first minute to last. The 0-0 draw left Celtic with a massive hill to climb in Madrid and two late goals for the Spaniards deprived Stein's side of a final against Bayern Munich.

That would be the last time for 29 years Celtic would reach a European semi. The decade ended with a mini revival as Celtic reached a European Cup quarter-final against Real Madrid but despite a 2-0 first-leg win, McNeill's side lost 3-0 in Spain.

BACK FOR SECONDS John Hughes clashes with Leeds No.1 Gary Sprake, top, in the famous 2-1 win that lines up another final with Feyenoord but despite Jimmy Johnstone's best efforts, right, it's Rinus Israel, above, who is the winning skipper, not Billy McNeill in the 1970 European Cup final

ENDS IN TEARS Willie Wallace comes agonisingly close for Celts in final, top, and there's more heartache at full-time as McNeill is left ...died and bruised while Evan Williams congratulates Feyenoord's Wim Hanegem and boss Jock Stein feels the pain more than most, right

BRAWL GAME Atletico Madrid's Ruben Ayala is sent packing by referee Dogan Babacan during the 0-0 European Cup semi-final at Celtic Park in April 1974, right, and below, a brawl breaks out between the players at the tunnel at full time, while bottom, Jimmy Johnstone and Adelardo are kept apart by the Turkish whistler

PACKING A PUNCH
Olympiakos keeper Panagiotis Kelesidis clears his lines during a 1-1 draw at Celtic Park in September 1974

NO THROUGH ROAD Dixie Deans, comes close during Celtic's 0-0 home draw with Vejle in October 1973

AULD ONES ARE THE BEST Billy McNeill, goal hero Bertie Auld, Tommy Gemmell and Bobby Murdoch celebrate after a 3-0 European Cup first leg quarter-final win over Fiorentina in March 1970 while Jimmy Johnstone, above, is denied by Atletico Madrid keeper Miguel Reina in Parkhead draw in semi-final of European Cup four years later

36

CELTIC
EUROPEAN ADVENTURES

THE SEVENTIES

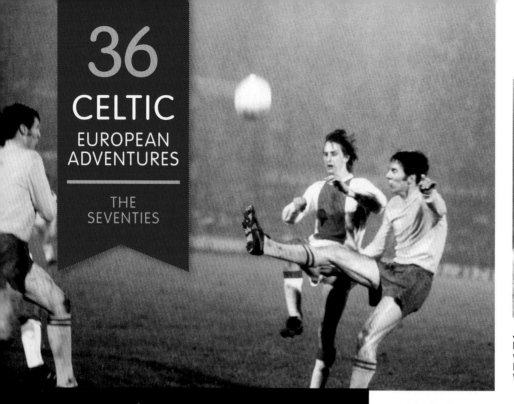

JOHAN AND JOHANNES Dutch master Cruyff helps Ajax dump Celts out of the 1971 European with a 3-0 triumph in Amsterdam, left, before Hoops star Edvaldsson, above, nets in 3-1 Cup Winners' Cup win over Boavista at Parkhead in 1

DECLINE OF THE TIMES Olympiakos hold Celtic to a 1-1 draw at Parkhead, above left, before knocking the Hoops out of the 1974 European Cup in Gree and Ronny McDonald celebrates his leveller against Wilsa Krakow, above, in 2-2 draw on home soil before the Poles win the UEFA Cup return 2-0 in 1976

EASY DOES IT
Joe Craig blasts home in a 5-0 first leg European Cup win over Jeunesse d'Esch in 1977 before Brian McLaughlin celebrates sealing the rout, right

THE FOUR AMIGOS
A young Tommy Burns takes on Wisla, above, and joins Dom Sullivan, Davie Provan and Johnny Doyle, left, in preparing for a trip to the Bernabeu in 1980, a game Celtic lose 3-0 to bow out of the European Cup after winning 2-0 at Parkhead

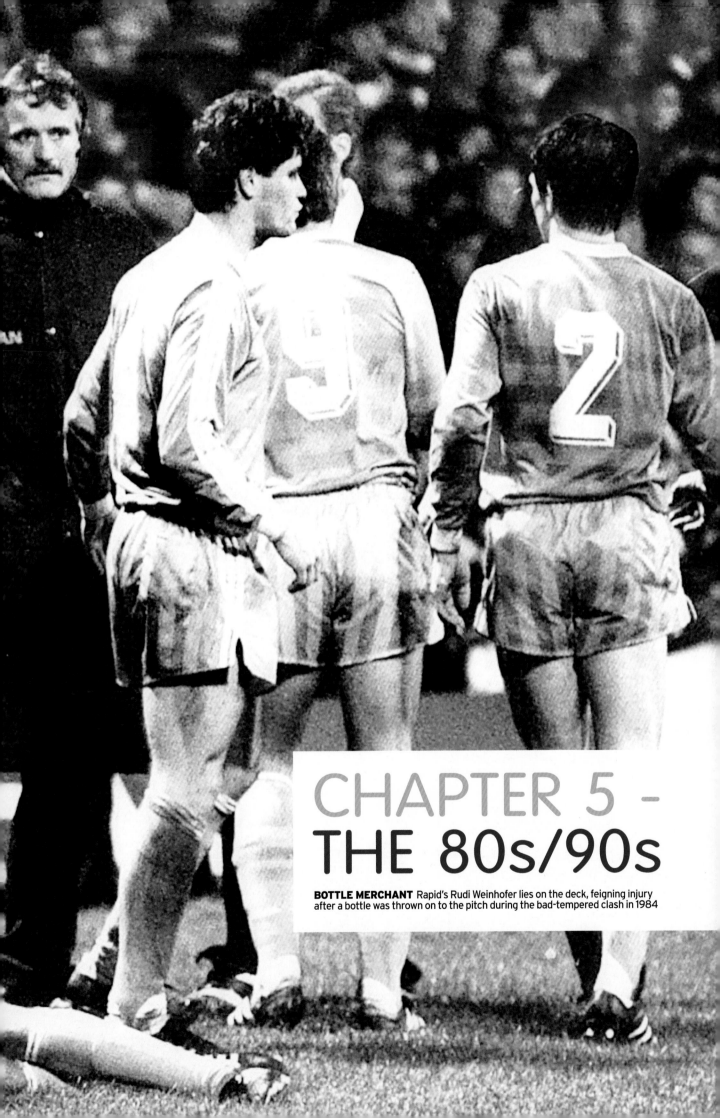

CHAPTER 5 -
THE 80s/90s

BOTTLE MERCHANT Rapid's Rudi Weinhofer lies on the deck, feigning injury after a bottle was thrown on to the pitch during the bad-tempered clash in 1984

CELTIC

EUROPEAN ADVENTURES

THE 80s/90s

REAL THRILLER
Murdo MacLeod
hails Johnny
Doyle after he put
Celts 2-0 up
against Real
Madrid in 1980
European Cup
quarter-final and
Bobby Lennox,
below, tries a shot

ITALIAN JOB
Tommy Burns, second left, is foiled by Juventus' Massimo Bonini but it's joy for the Hoops, above, as Charlie Nicholas wheels away to celebrate Murdo MacLeod scoring the only goal of the 1981 first-leg clash while Tom McAdam, left, gets stuck in

THE 80s and 90s brought the best and worst of times for Celtic in continental action and while there would be no shot at a European title there were mighty blows landed to bloody some of the biggest noses in the game.

And there are none bigger than Real Madrid, who came to Celtic Park on March 5, 1980 in the European Cup quarter-finals. To add extra spice, Madrid had turned out in an unfamiliar all-blue strip but two late goals from George McCluskey and Johnny Doyle sent the 67,000 full house wild.

Sadly, Celtic slid to defeat in the second leg but if the Madrid night at Parkhead was a spectacular high, the crushing low of the decade came four years later against Rapid Vienna. After going down 3-1 in the Cup Winners' Cup second round first leg, Celtic stormed the Austrians at a roaring Celtic Park in the return. But with Celts 3-0 up, bedlam erupted as Rapid put the boot in and one halfwit home fan lost the plot.

A bottle was tossed on to the park and Rapid's Rudi Weinhofer went down as if he had been shot. The bottle had landed five yards away from him but UEFA ordered a replay at Old Trafford and on a night marred by crowd trouble Celtic lost 1-0.

The following season UEFA forced the Hoops to play their Cup Winners' Cup first-round tie against Atletico Madrid behind closed doors. After an excellent 1-1 draw in Spain Celtic lost the second leg 2-1 to crash out.

Two ties stand out in the near 20-year absence from Europe's top table during the 80s and 90s – Sporting Lisbon in 1983 and Cologne in 1992. The Hoops turned in one of their finest home displays of any era on November 2, 1983. Trailing 2-0 from the UEFA Cup second round first leg in Portugal, Celtic dismantled Jozef Venglos's Sporting 5-0.

Nine years later, Cologne met a similar fate. After a 2-0 defeat in Germany, Celtic thumped their rivals 3-0 at Celtic Park in the decade's only real European high point.

DUTCHY FEELY Ajax boss Aad de Mos embraces Johan Cruyff, below, after the Dutch giants draw 2-2 at Celtic in 1982 where Davie Moyes, left, steams into tackle on Edo Ophof. Keeper Pat Bonner, below left, holds an inquest after the Bhoys lose a goal to Real Sociedad in previous round

BLAST FROM PAST Murdo MacLeod nets in a 2-1 UEFA Cup defeat to Nottingham Forest at Parkhead in December 1983

RAPID EXIT With Celtic going through to the third round of the Cup Winners' Cup 4-3 on aggregate, Rapid Vienna captain Hans Krankl attempts to lead his team off at Celtic Park in November 1984 after Rudolf Weinhofer pretended to be hit with a bottle, left, while manager Otto Baric gets in on the act, right

REPLAY BLOW Peter Grant hails Murdo MacLeod, below, after he scores the second goal in Celtic's 3-0 win over Rapid Vienna. However, despite an epic 4-3 aggregate win UEFA ordered a play-off in December 1984 at Old Trafford due to the bottle incident and Peter Pacult rounded Pat Bonner to net the only goal, above, before a fan ran on and pushed the Austrian side's keeper Herbert Feurer into the back of the net, below right

A TRUE GENT Frank McGarvey nets in a 3-0 win over Gent in the Cup Winners' Cup first round in October 1984

GHOST GAME Mo Johnston in action against Atletico Madrid in October 1985 in a 2-1 Cup Winners' Cup defeat played behind closed doors at Parkhead in the wake of the Rapid Vienna fiasco at Old Trafford

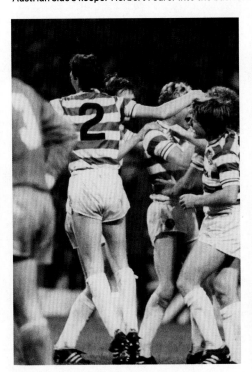

GLORIOUS FAILURE
Dariusz "Jacki" Dziekanowski celebrates netting
his fourth goal against Partizan Belgrade in the
1989 Cup Winners' Cup but the Hoops still bow out
in the first round on away goals after a thrilling
5-4 win at Parkhead makes it 6-6 on aggregate

**SWEET SMELL
OF SUCCESS**
John Collins take
the fight to Colo
as Celtic claw ba
a 2-0 deficit with
thrilling 3-0 win
Parkhead in the
1992 UEFA Cup

E BAT CAVE Dinamo Batumi's fans whip up torm, left, as Celts win 3-2 in the 1995 Cup nners' Cup before Andy Thom nets in a 4-0 at home, below. But the run is ended by PSG er Pierre van Hooijdonk misses in Paris, top

CADETE RECRUIT Jorge Cadete clashes with Pat Bonner as Sporting Lisbon knock Celts out of the 1993 UEFA Cup, above, but he then pulls on the Hoops and scores in a 1-0 UEFA Cup win over Kosice in 1996, left

SEE YOU SOON Alan Stubbs battles future Celtic star Mark Viduka as the Hoops lose a Champions League qualifier to Dinamo Zagreb in 1998, left, after Gerry Creaney fails to stop Borussia Dortmund from ending the 1992 UEFA Cup run, above, with a 2-1 victory at Parkhead

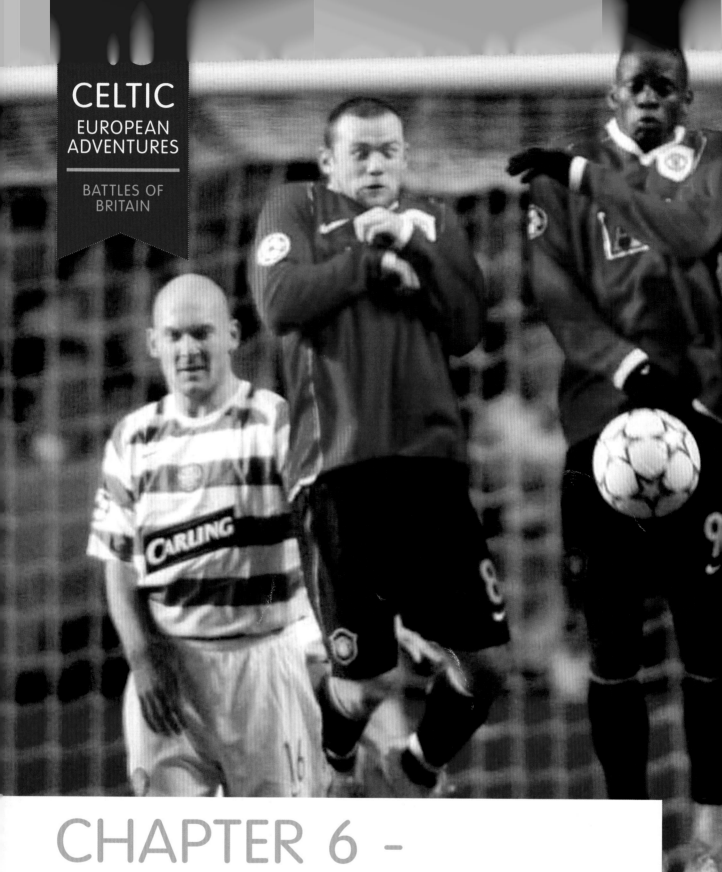

CELTIC
EUROPEAN
ADVENTURES

BATTLES OF
BRITAIN

CHAPTER 6 –
BATTLES OF BRITAIN

THE RISING SUN With less than 10 minutes left to play, Japanese playmaker Shunsuke Nakamura unleashes a brilliant 30-yard free-kick to secure a 1-0 win for Celtic against Manchester United that clinches a place in the Champions League last 16 for the first time

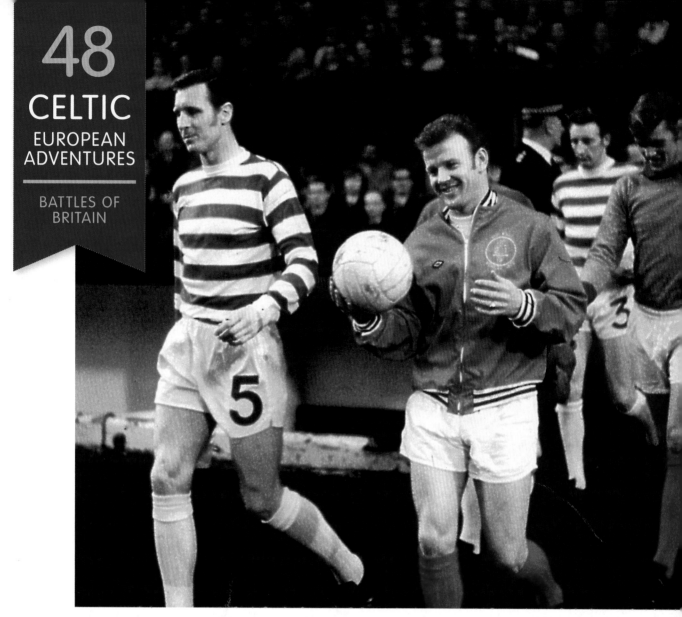

FEW showdowns get the pulses racing like a battle of Britain and Celtic hearts have been all a flutter through the decades when they have been at their brilliant best dispatching teams from across the border.

Pulling Celtic from the hat in Europe hasn't worked out well for many an English team... Just ask Don Revie's Leeds United.

The cataclysmic European Cup semi-final in 1970 set the standard for cross-border battles as Jock Stein's side put the mighty English champions to the sword not once but twice on two unforgettable ties in April 1970.

After a 1-0 away win Celtic reached the final with a magnificent 2-1 win at a packed Hampden as Jimmy Johnstone ran riot, destroying United stalwarts Norman Hunter

and Terry Cooper. Hunter later admitted in his autobiography that Stein's Celtic team were the best he had ever faced.

Martin O'Neill's arrival as manager in July 2000 created a Celtic earthquake and the aftershocks are still being felt even now.

Domestically brilliant, he gave the club back its pride on the European stage too and this was never more evident during the 2003 run to the UEFA Cup final.

Two English sides were sent packing, Blackburn Rovers in round two and Liverpool in the quarter-finals. Rovers came first and the tie was laced with controversy with former Rangers boss Graeme Souness occupying the Ewood Park dugout. After Celtic's narrow first-leg 1-0 win, Souness

claimed it was men against boys only for the Hoops to win 2-0 in the second leg.

Liverpool met a similar fate as another second-leg Rolls Royce performance from O'Neill's men resulted in another 2-0 win and John Hartson's clincher will live long in green and white memories.

Manchester United were next to feel the full force of Celtic Park on November 21 2006. Sir Alex Ferguson's men were hot favourites in the Champions League group tie but Shunsuke Nakamura's wonderful free-kick earned a 1-0 win and propelled Celtic into the knockout phase of the competition for the first time. Artur Boruc's late penalty save from Louis Saha was the icing on the cake as Parkhead went wild.

LEVELLER
John Hughes watches his header cross the line, left, as Celtic cancel out Bremner's 14th minute strike

READY FOR BATTLE Billy McNeill and Billy Bremner lead out the teams for the European Cup semi-final at Elland Road in 1970. Celtic take a 1-0 lead back to Glasgow thanks to George Connelly's strike in the first minute

ROAD TO THE FINAL Bobby Murdoch puts Celtic 2-1 up against Leeds, above. Bertie Auld celebrates, left, along with his team-mates as Celtic book their place in the European Cup Final

BHOYS BATTLE ON Celtic went to Ewood Park in November 2002 with a 1-0 lead over Blackburn Rovers from the first-leg. The Hoops booked their place in the third round of the UEFA Cup thanks to goals from Henrik Larsson, above left, and Chris Sutton, above right, in the retu...

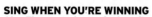

SING WHEN YOU'RE WINNING
Alan Thompson jumps for joy after his opener against Liverpool, top, then continues the celebrations at full-time with team-mate Joos Valgaeren. Neil Lennon also pulls on a Reds shirt after the game as he hails the travelling Hoops faithful

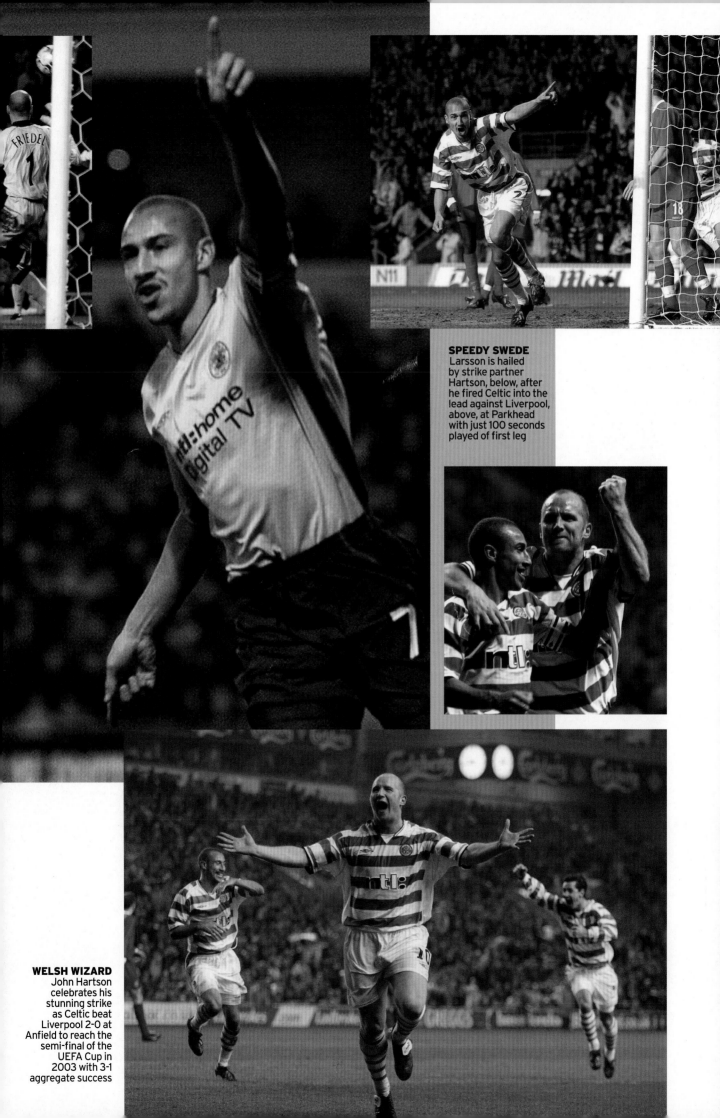

SPEEDY SWEDE
Larsson is hailed by strike partner Hartson, below, after he fired Celtic into the lead against Liverpool, above, at Parkhead with just 100 seconds played of first leg

WELSH WIZARD
John Hartson celebrates his stunning strike as Celtic beat Liverpool 2-0 at Anfield to reach the semi-final of the UEFA Cup in 2003 with 3-1 aggregate success

THEATRE OF DREAMS In 2006, Celtic were drawn alongside Manchester United in the Champions League group stages. Jan Vennegoor of Hesselink put Celtic ahead, top left, at Old Trafford before Saha equalised. Nakamura restored Hoops' lead top, but again Saha levelled. Ole Gunnar Solskjaer earned United the win but Celtic had their revenge with a 1-0 win in the return fixture at Parkhead, left

PARTY IN PARADISE Louis Saha's last-minute penalty is saved by Celtic keeper Artur Boruc, right, which sparks celebration between Hoops team-mates Jiri Jarosik and Thomas Gravesen, below

JAPAN-EASY Cristiano Ronaldo is closed down by the Celtic midfield, above. Nakamura celebrates, right, after his stunning 30-yard free-kick, below, 10 minutes from time earns Celtic a famous victory

POLE-AXED Boruc is hailed by his teammates, left, after his penalty save, while Kenny Miller and Gordon Strachan, above, celebrate from the sidelines

CHAPTER 7 – CHAMPIONS LEAGUE NIGHTS

DUTCH OF CLASS Bobby Petta slams home Celtic's opener in a 3-1 win at the Amsterdam ArenA in August 2001. The victory would propel Martin O'Neill's men into the group stages of the competition for the first time

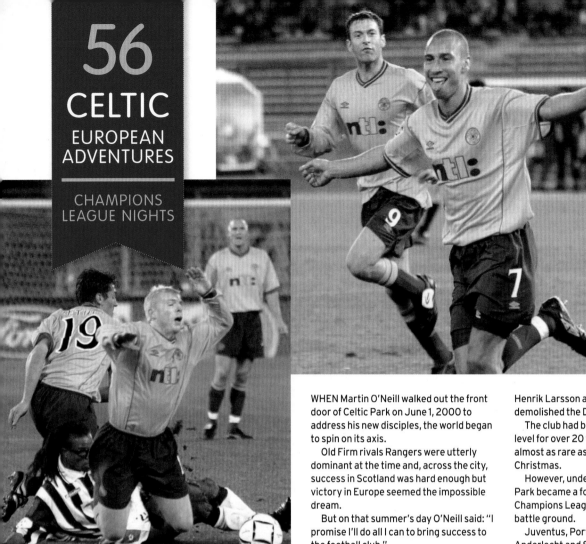

HEARTACHE Henrik Lars: thought he had earned Ce: point in Turin with a late p but Juve's Nicola Amoruse a controversial last-minut spot-kick and, left, Neil Le and Edgar Davids battle fo

WHEN Martin O'Neill walked out the front door of Celtic Park on June 1, 2000 to address his new disciples, the world began to spin on its axis.

Old Firm rivals Rangers were utterly dominant at the time and, across the city, success in Scotland was hard enough but victory in Europe seemed the impossible dream.

But on that summer's day O'Neill said: "I promise I'll do all I can to bring success to the football club."

He was true to his word as the Irishman delivered a first season treble - suddenly the Hoops were back at Europe's top table – a football feast followed.

Drawn against Ajax in the final qualifying round for the Champions League, the mission could not have been tougher.

But in a performance that would not have been out of place in the late 60s, O'Neill's new-look team spearheaded by

Henrik Larsson and Chris Sutton demolished the Dutch 3-1.

The club had been lost at Europe's top level for over 20 years with big wins almost as rare as appearances after Christmas.

However, under the Irishman, Celtic Park became a fortress and the Champions League became the club's battle ground.

Juventus, Porto, Rosenborg, Lyon, Anderlecht and Shaktar Donetsk were all put to the sword under O'Neill in Europe's top competition.

The UEFA Cup yielded a run for the ages in 2003 as O'Neill took them to within a whisker of silverware but in recent times nothing has set the pulses racing like the Champions League.

Celtic Park is now firmly established as one of world football's most intimidating arenas. The genesis of that was on the 1st of June in the year 2000.

IN THE THICK OF THE ACTION Celtic idol Lubo Moravcik battles for the ball during the home victory over Juventus in October 2001, the final match of the group campaign

SWEDE FINISH Henrik Larsson's first-half strike against Porto at Parkhead, above, earns Celtic their first Champions League points the 2001/02 group campaign and, left, Alan Thompson heads the opener against Bayern Munich in the first group game of 2003/04 but two goals from Roy Makaay sealed a home win for the Germans

C EXIT
utton celebrates
ond strike, below,
ic bow out of the
ions League in
2 with a 4-3 home
r Juventus

HART OF THE MATTER John Hartson beats Carles Puyol to the ball to head Celtic level at the Nou Camp in the group clash in November 2004 – the match with Barcelona ended 1-1

OVER AND OUT Celtic finish bottom of their group despite Alan Thompson's solitary strike giving them a 1-0 win over Shakhtar Donetsk, left, and Neil Lennon, above, playing his part in holding AC Milan to a goalless draw

LENNY LAPS IT UP Neil Lennon hails the fans as he walks off with Artur Boruc after a 3-0 win over Benfica in Group F in October 2006

THE ITALIAN JOB
Scott McDonald grabs a last-minute winner in Group D as Celtic beat holders AC Milan 2-1 at Parkhead in October 2007 and, below, Scott Brown gets stuck on Czech star Marek Jankulovski

SWEET 16 Kenny Miller nets a penalty, above left, in a 1-0 win over Copenhagen in Group F in 2006, the striker then hit a brace against Benfica, above, while Stephen Pearson got the other, left, in a 3-0 win with Gordon Strachan's side later reaching the last-16 for the first time. And in February 2008 they were in the last-16 again with Vennegoor of Hesselink scoring, right in a 3-2 defeat to Barca

ON THE SPOT McDonald celebrates, main pic, after putting Celtic ahead in the qualifier against Spartak Moscow in August 2007. The Hoops eventually beat the Russians 4-3 on penalties to reach the group stages

GROUP AID Aiden McGeady takes on Clarence Seedorf as Celtic lose 1-0 at AC Milan in their final Group D game in December 2007 but they qualify for the last 16 for the second year in a row thanks to Benfica's victory at Shakhtar Donetsk

DANE PAIN Shaun Maloney wins a penalty against Aalborg in September 2008, above, only for Robson to miss in a 0-0 draw while Aiden McGeady takes on Darren Fletcher, above middle, as Celtic crash to a 3-0 defeat at Man United a month later in Group E

WATT A FEELING
Striker Tony Watt celebrates putting Celtic 2-0 up against Barcelona in the Champions League group stages in November 2012, after Victor Wanyama had nodded home the opener, below

HISTORIC NIGHT Celtic boss Lennon is overcome with emotion after his side's famous 2-1 win, above, as dejected Barca star Javier Mascherano leaves the field

FLYING START Gary Hooper powers home a header to put Celtic in front against Spartak Moscow after just 12 minutes in the Luzhniki Stadium, October 2012

LATE SHOW A last-gasp header from Georgios Samaras , above, earns Celtic a historic first away win in Champions League group stages as Hoops beat Spartak 3-2 in Russia

NO REPEAT PERFORMANCE Celtic can't earn another famous win against Barca, below, as Spanish giants win 1-0

CHAPTER 8 - SEVILLE

JUMPING FOR BHOYS Celtic fans gear up a party in Seville as the clock ticks down to their date with destiny at the 2003 UEFA Cup final – more than 80,000 made the trip to the Spanish city to see their heroes take on Porto, the club's first European final since 1970

CELTIC
EUROPEAN ADVENTURES

SEVILLE

FINAL TOUCH
Henrik Larsson nets in the 1-0 win away to Boavista that took Celtic to Seville, above

DATELINE: Basel. August 28, 2002, 9.28pm. One dream dies and another begins as Celtic take their first steps on the Road to Seville in depressing circumstances.

A shock exit from the final qualifying round of the Champions League was a bitter pill to swallow for Martin O'Neill's men.

But no one could have guessed it would give birth to the sweet taste of European glory and a rollercoaster ride all the way to the UEFA Cup Final in Spain.

Led by talisman Henrik Larsson, Celtic took on and beat some of the best teams the continent had to offer.

A 10-1 first-round aggregate win over Suduva was no indicator of the epic tussles that were to follow. But a blockbuster tie in round two against a Blackburn side bossed by ex-Rangers boss Graeme Souness suddenly sparkled the UEFA Cup to life and the fans began to

dream again of Euro glory.

Rovers were dispatched, then Celta Vigo as O'Neill secured European football for the club for the first time after Christmas in 23 years.

Stuttgart were blown away in a sensational fourth-round tie – the final 5-4 aggregate scarcely doing justice to a pulsating 180 minutes which saw Celtic storm back from losing the first goal at home.

Liverpool looked favourites in the quarters after a 1-1 draw at Parkhead but the Hoops rose to the occasion at Anfield to win 2-0 and book a semi-final place.

It was just after Easter that Celtic dumped Boavista and a first European trophy since 1967 was within their grasp.

But in a sweltering Seville, Porto's despicable tactics emerged triumphant after Larsson's sensational double had the travelling army of 80,000 fans in raptures.

Jose Mourinho's team nicked the cup in extra-time but O'Neill had given Celtic their pride back on the big stage their fans craved.

THE BHOYS FROM SEVILLE Fans lap up the sun and the atmosphere as they descend en masse on Seville for the UEFA Cup final in May 2003. No one who was there will ever forget the buzz of the Spanish city as the Hoops supporters filled the streets, bars and squares and even though Celtic were pipped by Porto it truly was a fan fiesta like no other

GLORY BHOYS Larsson puts the Hoops ahead in their 1-1 home draw with Liverpool, left, while above Stilyan Petrov makes it 3-1 against Stuttgart at Celtic Park and, below, Neil Lennon and Rab Douglas celebrate the 2-0 away win over Blackburn Rovers

SPAIN GAIN John Hartson, above, smashes home the vital goal in the 2-1 defeat by Celta Viga in Spain which took the Hoops through on away goals while, left, Joos Valgaeren nets in 8-1 win home win over Suduva of Lithuania with Chris Sutton looking on

SEA OF GREEN AND WHITE
Neil Lennon, manager Martin O'Neill, John Kennedy and Liam Miller take to the pitch before kick to soak up the atmosphere at packed Estadio La Cartuja ahead of the UEFA Cup final in 2003, with Hoops fans unveiling a huge shirt banner in the stands, right

BOBO'S BOO-BOO
Porto's Deco writhes on the deck after being caught by Celtic defender Bobo Balde, left, and it's disaster for Celts as the big stopper is sent off for a second booking in extra time, below left, with Didier Agathe watching on

PUTTING THE BOOT IN
Celtic substitute Ulrik Laursen, who replaced Joos Valgaeren, tackles Porto keeper Vitor Baia, right, and Henrik Larsson gets stuck in to a challenge with Ricardo Costa, above

HAVING A BAWL Alan Thompson reacts furiously to time-wasting by Porto keeper Baia, on the deck, by screaming at referee Lubos Michel as both sets of players vent frustrations in a bad-tempered showpiece that often boiled over

HEAVEN AND HEARTACHE

Hero Larsson celebrates netting for the second time against Porto, left, but in the end it was agony for him, the Hoops and Celts fans as they went down 3-2 after extra time to the Portuguese side with O'Neill dejected after picking up a silver medal, right, as the players went on a lap of the pitch to salute gutted supporters, above

NOTHING LEFT Neil Lennon lays exhausted and defeated on the pitch in Seville, top, and it was agony in the stands for fans with knackered supporters crashing out at the airport ahead of a trip back to Glasgow

HOOPS INVASION Thousands of Celtic fans make their way throug[h] Seville in a stunning turnout for the travelling support who turned th[e] city green and white, above, with many heading to the *Daily Record* b[us] left, to join the party and pick up some special memorabilia

HOT ON THE TRAIL Hoops fans cool off in a water fountain while others don sombreros to keep the heat at bay in the brilliant Spanish sunshine ahead of the UEFA Cup final

NIGHTMARE
It's torture at the final whistle for the support, left, as the dream of another European trophy disappears but with so many fans heading to Seville and hotels crammed to capacity, some took to sleeping off the agony on the street, above

70

CELTIC

EUROPEAN
ADVENTURES

STRACHAN,
LENNON AND
THE BEATING
OF BARCA

CHAPTER 9 – STRACHAN, LENNON & THE BEATING OF BARCA

NIGHT TO REMEMBER Celtic fans create a wall of noise and colour as they prepare to face Barcelona in November, 2012

CELTIC can beat ANYONE in their Glasgow colosseum.

Not a piece of hyperbole, a statement of fact and Lionel Messi has the scars to prove it.

The football greats have passed through Parkhead's gates in these days of the money-talks Champions League but the passion of Celtic's pulsating Paradise has seen the pockets picked of many a rich man.

And none more so than Messi and his pals who arrived in November 2012 as the greatest club side the world had ever seen and left with a bloody nose delivered by Neil Lennon's London Road lions.

Goals from Victor Wanyama and Tony Watt sent shock waves around Europe and nearly blew the roof off Celtic Park.

Messi scored – the greats always do – but it was mere consolation on a night of nights in Glasgow's East End.

If reaching the summit of European football is now rendered almost impossible by the cascade of money flowing through a select few clubs from the world's biggest countries, Celtic have proved they can still live with the best.

As the Martin O'Neill era came to an end in 2005, Gordon Strachan had picked up the gauntlet and delivered his own brand of European success.

Two successive last-16 appearances in the Champions League for the first time ever wowed fans and media alike.

Strachan had seen off AC Milan, Benfica, Manchester United and Copenhagen en route to the knockout stages but dreadful draws against first Barcelona and then Milan put paid to any further progression.

Lennon set the gold standard for Fortress Paradise when he took over in the dugout and delivered that battering of Barca.

His side of Kris Commons, Gary Hooper and Joe Ledley marched to a date in the last 16 with Juventus in 2013 – another impressive bookmark in Celtic's European adventure.

COMMON GROUND Kris Commons battles with Jordi Alba and, below, Tony Watt celebrates with Charlie Mulgrew after he bags the second goal

WATT A GUY
Tony Watt blasts home his historic winner v Barca while Mulgrew's strike is blocked by Bartra at Celtic Park

VICTOR-Y DANCE Victor Wanyama congratulated the Celtic players including Joe Ledley, Charlie Mulgrew, Adam Matthews and Miku after he broke deadlock at Parkhead in November 2012 with the goal proving to be crucial as the Hoops went on to create a piece of history

CATALAN COLLAPSE It was a different story against Barcelona a few weeks before as the Hoops lost 2-1 despite a valiant effort with Fraser Forster pulling off saves from Lionel Messi and Neil Lennon, right, was left distraught but the players still received some well-earned applause at the end of an exhilarating match

IF YOU KNOW THE HISTORY Parkhead history was made as Lionel Messi, above, and co were put to the sword by Neil Lennon's side and the Hoops gaffer was not slow in coming on to the pitch to congratulate his players, including Joe Ledley, left

CELTIC
EUROPEAN ADVENTURES

STRACHAN, LENNON AND THE BEATING OF BARCA

SOMETHING SPECIAL
Shunsuke Nakamura is hailed by Shaun Maloney after his free-kick winner against Manchester United in 2006, Stephen Pearson celebrates the third goal in 3-0 win over Benfica, top right, skipper Stephen McManus is thrilled with opener in 2-1 win over AC Milan, middle, and Scott McDonald slides on his knees with Paul Hartley in tow after celebrating early strike in 1-1 draw with United in 2008

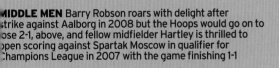

MIDDLE MEN Barry Robson roars with delight after strike against Aalborg in 2008 but the Hoops would go on to lose 2-1, above, and fellow midfielder Hartley is thrilled to open scoring against Spartak Moscow in qualifier for Champions League in 2007 with the game finishing 1-1

CHAPTER 10 -
THE FANS

BILLY IDOL Greatest Ever Celtic skipper Billy McNeill greets the crowd at a fanzone in Seville ahead of the 2003 UEFA Cup final. McNeill skippered the club in their previous European showpiece, in 1970 against Feyenoord

BEST FANS BAR NONE
Supporters set off from the Glenbervie Bar in the Gorbals in the back of a van ahead of the European Cup final in Milan against Feyenoord in May 1970 while dedicated duo Peter Fyfe and Stevie Gunn, left, make a pilgrimage to the Estadio Nacional in Lisbon ahead of the Champions League clash with Benfica in November 2012

RECORD CROWD
Daily Record competition winners prepare to fly out to Milan for 1970 final

SAIL, SAIL THE CELTS ARE HERE
Supporters board a ferry, below, as they head to Italy

HAIL CESAR Billy McNeill with autograph hunters at Renfrew Airport in September 1965 before the 6-0 win in Holland in the Cup Winners' Cup first-round match against Go Ahead Eagles

GET INTER THEM Celtic Park is full of expectant fans, left and above, in April 1972 for the European Cup semi-final second leg against Inter Milan. The match ended 0-0 after a scoreless draw in the first match with the Italians winning 5-4 on penalties

MAD FOR IT Johnny Doyle, top, and Charlie Nicholas, centre-right, join fans in Madrid ahead of the European Cup quarter-final with Real in March 1980. Doyle scored in the 2-0 first-leg win but Celtic lost 3-0 at the Bernabeu

MOUS FANS Elizabeth Taylor and Richard ...ton throw a party for 5000 supporters in ...ngary after the 2-1 win over Ujpest Dozsa in ... European Cup quarter-final in March 1972

HEROES TO SIROS Dejected fans outside San Siro after 2-1 defeat to Feyenoord in the European Cup final

82

CELTIC
EUROPEAN
ADVENTURES

THE FANS

SUNNY DELIGHT Fans party in Seville as they watch the big game

CLASH OF TITANS The Celtic fans hope they are heading to Wembley for the Champions League final in 2013 but a 3-0 home loss to Juventus in the last-16 first-leg clash in February ended the dream

RALLYING CRY The Celtic fans give a message to to the players ahead of the 2-2 Europa League Group A draw with Fenerbahce in October 2015

SWITCHED ON SUPPORT Fans recall the legendary 1967 final as Celtic take on old rivals Inter Milan in the Europa League last-32 in February 2015 with the Parkhead crowd enjoying a 3-3 thriller

FINAL DELIVERY Fans in Milan are handed copies of the *Daily Record* by Sylvia Skillcorn and Mary Baker, right, ahead of the European Cup final in 1970